This Coloring Book Belongs To

Color Test Page

Afghan Hound

Akita

Alaskan Malamute

Australian Cattle

Bichon Frise

Bernese Mountain

Berger Picard

Beagle

Basenji

Australian Shepherd

Border Collie

Boston Terrier

Boxer

Bulldog

Bullmastiff

Chihuahua

Cocker Spaniel

Great Dane

Maltese

Pomeranian

Samoyed

Siberian Husky

Dachshund

Great Pyrenees

Mastiff

Poodle

Scottish Terrier

Stafordshire Bull Terrier

Dalmatian

Greyhound

Miniature Schnauzer

Portuguese Water

Shetland Sheepdog

Weimaraner

Doberman Pinscher

Havanese

Newfoundland

Rhodesian Ridgeback

Shiba Inu

Whippet

German Shepherd

Irish Setter

Papillon

Rottweiler

Shih Tzu

Yorkshire Terrier

Golden Retriever

Labrador Retriever

Pembroke Welsh Corgi

Saint Bernard

Share with your friends through feedback!

Help someone you've never met, even if you never got credit for it.
Who is this person you ask? They are like you. They Love Coloring Books. Share your enthusiasm and fun with coloring books by leaving a review to help people find the coloring books you enjoy!
Most people do, in fact, judge a book by its cover (and its reviews). So here's my ask on behalf of a struggling Coloring Book Enthusiasts you've never met:
Please help that Colorist by leaving this book a review.
Your gift costs no money and less than 60 seconds to make real, but can change a fellow Colorist's life forever. Your review could help...
...one more small businesses provide for their community.
...one more entrepreneur support their family.
...one more employee get meaningful work.
...one more Colorist transform their life.
...one more dream come true.
To get that 'feel good' feeling and help this person for real, all you have to do is...and it takes less than 60 seconds...

LEAVE A REVIEW

Thank you from the bottom of my heart.
- Your biggest fan, Janice.

www.ingramcontent.com/pod-product-compliance
Lightning Source LLC
LaVergne TN
LVHW081416110826
845149LV00010B/1762

* 9 7 9 8 9 8 9 7 4 5 0 1 2 *